"Harold J. Recinos's *Tell Somebody* is a remarkable triumph. The collection of poetry is a deeply contemplative and poignant exploration of pressing societal themes, including poverty, injustice, and grief. Recinos conjures a vivid and unforgettable portrait of life on the margins, where laborers carry the scent of shattered dreams and are forgotten by mainstream society. Amidst the darkness, Recinos also celebrates the beauty of life and the resilience of the human spirit, creating a work that shines like a constellation of stars and a flock of pigeons taking flight"

—RUBEN QUESADA
professor of writing, Antioch University

"The poet sees, hears, feels, remembers, and answers the call to 'tell somebody.' These are poems of nostalgia for a city with streets 'where paradise was felt,' poems of rage toward the empire with its 'conquest, wars / greed, stories, legislators, judges,' poems of bewilderment at 'the intolerable silence / of God.' But ultimately, they are poems of love for the disinherited and hope for a light to shine again in the 'earth-shattering darkness' of the present."

—MELANIE NICHOLSON
professor Spanish and Latin American literature, Bard College

"In *Tell Somebody*, Harold Recinos takes us on a profound journey through the streets of New York, the beaches of Puerto Rico, and the campos of Central America. He reminds us of beautiful children, failed by adults, schools, and churches; migrants who cross dangerous spaces, only to be rejected because of color and language. Read these deeply thoughtful poems by a passionate advocate and come in touch with authentic humanity so you can indeed *Tell Somebody*!"

—EFRAIN AGOSTO
distinguished visiting professor in Latina/o studies, Williams College

"With tremendous heart and hurt, Harold Recinos writes poems that focus the reader on how we fail one another as human beings, and also on how we might live differently, with more empathy, love, and hope. Such is the essential challenge to readers of *Tell Somebody*."

—Seth Michelson
associate professor of Spanish, Washington and Lee University

"In Harold Recinos's urgent, new collection, *Tell Somebody,* we find poems compelled by cultural crisis to forge connection, to mend afflictions born of difference, to speak the news across not only antinomies within and beyond oneself, but also 'the gap separating the fingertip / of God and Adam.' These are poems both unflinching in their attentions and resilient in their prospective aspirations and resolve."

—Bruce Bond
professor of English, University of North Texas

Tell Somebody

Tell Somebody

HAROLD J. RECINOS

RESOURCE *Publications* • Eugene, Oregon

TELL SOMEBODY

Resource Publications
An Imprint of Wipf and Stock Publishers
199 W. 8th Ave., Suite 3
Eugene, OR 97401

www.wipfandstock.com

PAPERBACK ISBN: 978-1-6667-7512-9
HARDCOVER ISBN: 978-1-6667-7513-6
EBOOK ISBN: 978-1-6667-7514-3

06/28/23

Contents

DEAR LANGSTON

the city is the East River
where the poor speak at all
hours of hot summer days.
the city is old tenements
where grandmothers scribble
letters for mixed family that
are never sent. the city is the
street mouthing in Spanglish
wounds in prayer and probing
faces. the city is a short walk past
your old row house apartment in
Harlem, the Puerto Rican flags on
fire escapes a couple of blocks over
and exiled Cubans and Salvadorans
in your Harlem Renaissance. the city
is the supreme place on aging earth
where the poor bend passing hours
held closely in gossiped dreams.

THE KIDS

I write for the kids whose
bodies are limp on rooftops
where they gasp their last
breath, high. I shout about
the Black and Brown boys
and girls that lived too short
a time while the downtown
crowd looked away. I look
up at heaven naming people
who have grown up on tears
in a world where justice has
never been colorblind.

LIFTED UP

the memories never wither
like cut flowers on the fifth
floor window sill facing the
street. you are the little kid
climbing the mango tree, the
boy sitting on high branches,
a strong wind rustling leaves,
the barefoot child running on grass
in a Jamaican yard, a starched
uniform for 2nd grade, tears without
words of complaint, a body more
wilted each year and too worn out
in bed to dream. you are crosses
placed on subway platforms, votive
candles beneath the Big Pun Mural,
life experienced like numbered days
and the one who died an untimely
death. you are the youth who fell in
rich men's wars, the tortured priests
who defended you, mortally wounded
parents too poor for love and church
bells calling people to pray. you are the
same old story we tell on the street that
makes single mothers cry, the eyes that
keep watch and memories that bathe us
with love.

STARS

we go to school every day to
learn a little more English from
story books written by people
trafficking their experience of
the world into Spanglish heads
and boasting about their feelings
that will never start a fire in the
neighborhood's wherever pigeons
branch on the edges of fire escapes
with dark eyes summoning many
of the Spanglish thoughts rambling
in us. the old white teachers believing
they are doing their best have not walked
miles down these streets like us shaking
their heads. the mystery of the life talked
about by mothers who gather nights to say
Spanish prayers to la Virgen de Guadalupe
clears the indigestion left by public school
and permits tears nesting in us to come out
of hiding like undocumented people taking
Holy Communion. we go to schools learning
to pledge allegiance to a flag draped over a
history that frankly never leans over to ask
our names!

THE BARRIO

it is dawn in the noisy
city and you sit in silence
eating yesterday's bread
picturing footprints in the
desert you crossed. you have
a rosary implored in the darkest
part of night that weeps with
you. you are the girl walking
the sidewalk giggling at a clarinet
player on the corner with a hat
waiting for change. you are songs
from birds gathered in the little
park washing cracked souls with
endless hope. you are the candles
burning in a church to bring miracles
to the street for those whose tears fall
on sidewalks.

RETURNED

she returned just months ago
after stumbling on the sidewalks
of English named streets, and still
a dreamer. her noisy cries splintered
trees with stories of the DACA life
and the journey back to a land she
never knew. the North was her home,
the palm trees things she had never seen
first hand and this Mesoamerican city a
grave for girls' dreams. nothing is equal in
America for the DACA youth asking in
the one language they deeply know where
do we belong? the country has received
her in a season of hope, it has embraced
her halting Spanish, an indigenous priest
and widows in his church now offer up
prayers for America's rejected Dreamer
to a speechless God with words found
no doubt in the first cave of visions in
the new world. she was just a child in
her mother's arms that wandered on foot,
bus and then trains into the land of purple
mountain majesty. her mother now rests
forever in California earth and today this
young girl entering a new darkness told me
she will not be broken despite the sadness
in her and hope will endure on the tip of her
tongue until time learns to speak it.

EMPIRE

the empire will disappear, its
wealth carried into timeless
oblivion, its conquests, wars,
greed, stories, legislators, judges,
white faced politicians and bloody
monuments will surrender power to
swallowing earth. the boots will be
lifted from every dark neck, chains
will scatter into fragments across the
world and heavenly grace will appear
on the new day to escort the wretched
to a splendid light. the empires impertinent
fathers will not resurrect, the underworld
will keep them trapped and the meek
will inherit God's earth. the empire will
perish, its pretentious permanence will
break like doors falling from hinges and
its victories one-by-one will not withstand
final judgement from upstairs. the desperate
repetitions of power will become nothing
more than dust and those who delighted in
the suffering of the weak will be distinctly
forgotten.

REVERSE STANDARD VERSION

you will never read in your theology
books or in the latest Revised Standard
version Bible that the Galilean Jesus has
set his people free in the South Bronx
though Puerto Ricans and Salvadorans
have been praying and genuflecting in that
borough for decades. we all know Jesus
did not witness four murders by the time he
was 11 like Tito who rides the subway into
Manhattan to work mopping floors, emptying
trash and cleaning toilets. Jesus never limped
down Westchester Avenue, heard the toll bells
ringing funeral rites for little Julia who shot so
much dope into her thirteen-year-old veins her
body was sent to Golgotha. you will have to
look for evidence that everlasting light shines
on the people that work seven days a week for
two days' pay, that live poor, die without a cent
and are called undeserving spics. the only thing
you might read for certain in your holy book
translated into more languages than Jesus himself
could speak is that God got everything wrong in
the South Bronx and the people down here spend
their days anxiously waiting for nothing more than
a simple blessing from the divine figure who they
believe speaks to the soul but in real life keeps not
saying a damn thing.

ESCAPE

she collected the most cherished
things to carry, pictures that would
fit in an envelope, memories in a
notebook, a tiny Bible and put on
clothes to keep her invisible in the
weeks long flight. she determined
to leave behind a world of violence
to carry with her the faces of women
that strengthened her will to live even
in the shadows that hid her frail body
and fears. she prayed that night to her
impoverished God pleading with the
mute to deliver her to a place of hiding
in the North, untouched by the crimes
of executioners dressed in uniforms
and where the victims of Herod in the
lived world could whisper after lament
from tears in their ghostly eyes fell to
earth your flight is rescue. she made it
to the city of onlookers, the asylum of
women and children from the land she
fled and to the building where a cousin
waited after too many days of lighting
candles and saying prayers to persuade
God to help.

ENLIGHTENMENT

the way we live, think, act,
and note what matters troubles
your world. the racist theories
in your reasoning, your dialectical
philosophy that calls us brutes and
dark-skinned thugs are enlightenment
views chaining us to trees and hanging
us to death by the neck. your institutions
of learning have failed to confess for
generations the knowledge they shaped
with ignorance, their discourses of
superior whiteness, their steadfast
disapproval of non-white knowing.
the words your theologians offered
to justify violence and dispossession,
their razor thin morality and white Jesus
have turned us into Caliban on this land
stolen by European hands in the name
of a twisted God. someday, you will know
heaven is debating a final verdict for the
wickedness your civilization has given its
darker brothers and sisters on earth.

MUSIC

before music on the block
silence was quoted by the
streets, dancing was not in
use, smiles were quite rare
and kids waited to play. before
music yesterday was flat, the
weariness held on and not even
a note pierced darkness with
song. then, salsa came out of
a building played by a curly haired
young man slapping congas with
trumpets announcing joy right
behind him and the world changed.

BIG PUN

I walked past the empty church
to the curve in the road where the
subway stops before crawling back
into a dark tunnel that welcomes its
light. the old men at their spots on
a corner who had archived the truth
in their souls when young gathered
on folding chairs to talk for the day
about how much less they knew of
the world. when I overheard them,
it occurred to me I would love to know
less about the world that needs to use
the word spic and why English language
dictionaries list it. the last time I visited
the empty church was for the memorial
held to pay tribute to the kid we all knew
who overdosed on heroin on a rooftop on
Intervale Avenue, his mother said Joey
was in a better place, and those of us who
dropped out of junior high school with him
could hardly keep up with that mystery of
faith. I had a few more blocks to reach the
Wall with a mural of Big Pun, the first Latino
rapper to go platinum, who now rests in peace
collecting flowers, candles, and votive prayers
from the neighborhood poor who believe the
rapper speaks to God for them. I got to the wall
and left the player from the hood fresh cut
flowers!

THE INHERITANCE

I have one photograph of me
posed on a step leading into a
South Bronx alley aged just a
year. the Puerto Ricans were
moving to the block, working
the factories on the other side
of the little creek and cracked
windows were not decorating
tenements. you cannot see then
the look on my face that followed
me around when people said your
Guatemalan father makes you half
Boricua, others whispered you are
not Indian enough and America did
not hesitate to call me spic. by the
time I learned to speak my mother's
Spanish, a world of strangers became
my common tongue on that block that
talked little to families left behind or
kept pictures in old shoe boxes that
begged decent burials. I became an
altar boy in the church that baptized
me, never heard a Mass said in English
and thought God best have saved a whole
lot of tears up for mixed race kids like
me.

THE CATHEDRAL

you stayed up last night looking
at pictures of the Holy land that
is south of the border, the place
that does not speak the language
of Christ, the one all the poets in
exile for nearly a century have not
let disappear in places imagining
peace, the crying land where your
sister died too young near the village
with dissent songs. sometimes, we
wonder how important it is for others
to say the name of a country full of
tears, grandmothers who pray for children
on the other side, and people who confess
belief in God yet never hesitated to nail the
poor to the cross. we paused viewing a photo
of the Cathedral of the martyred Bishop who
was never quiet about the beautiful and ugly
in life and I could not help saying in a loud
voice that the gap separating the finger tip
of God and Adam in Michelangelo's Creation
of Adam is the space where most of the nation
that paid for the murder of a Saint lives each
day.

NEVER FORGET

do you recall the cantor in the
storefront Jewish temple on
Westchester Avenue who knew
far too much about light fading
away. remember the watch fixer
with numbers on his arm who
walked the South Bronx pavement
reciting Kaddish in whispers. I can
still see the Jewish lady who loved
to sit with the Puerto Rican kids on
the stoop on summer nights sharing
warmest memories and Yiddish sayings
that made the wind stall. I still think
about that time candles were lit on the
sidewalk in front of building 1203, the
old Jewish men and women held us by
the hand to recall with them what they
most craved to forget. it occurred to me
faced by the crimes of humanity that God
who made the world must ask each of us
for forgiveness.

THE CONSPIRACY

the Puerto Rican kids speak English
better than the white children in West
Virginia, many of them have the names
of Saints and they can rattle off lines from
Shakespeare plays. there is a conspiracy
to keep them invisible, to make sure they
fall down the rabbit holes in that little white
girl's wonderland, to never mention they
stood with King making his I have a Dream
speech and keeping them all lost in a black
and white world. there is a conspiracy to keep
silent about Brown brothers and sisters save to
call them illegitimate, to keep them at the
table reserved for the caged who no longer
sing of freedom, to call them pitiful spics and
keep them chained in US steel branded with
oppressive whiteness—I say bullshit!

WORN-OUT

I know you have heard something
about the themes repeated frequently
concerning what people around here
consider important to drag out of the
darkness and try to bargain for a tiny
miracle or chance of old fashioned
luck. the people sitting on the stoop
drinking cheap beer, listening to salsa
for hours, tired of packed apartments,
tiny furnished rooms, starvation wages,
pushing brooms and trembling on hot
summer days have dreams that exist
shorter than the beauty of cut flowers
sold in the bodega. sure, you may no
longer have an interest in the no good
coming out of this Nazareth, the parcels
from families south of here that are never
delivered by post, the tears of our children
banished from white playgrounds and the
simple needs that keep us gasping for life.
if you feel you are no longer able to think
about this side of the damn tracks, just
imagine how it is for the spat on poor who
think God is out of touch with the barrio
called trash.

WRINKLES

I saw time stretched out
on the newest wrinkles on
your grandmother's face
asking everyone to guess
what they mean. each line
was a story about years that
eagerly leaned forward with
words holding Sunday tightly.
the wind blew her long greying
hair covered by a black scarf and
the moment she smiled I looked
up in the direction of heaven to
pray about how dear to me was her
crinkled face. I knew by the way
she sat on the stoop that unlike Yeats
predicted of old age she was not full
of sleep.

REDEMPTION

I learned to live in dark times
before rotten divisions were
worthy of the nightly news,
in schools that called me spic,
in churches silent about daily
horrors on the street, in books
featuring a white history, days
in an apartment with too much
hunger, jumping across rooftops
to escape murderers and seeing
friends return in body bags from
war. I learned to live in darkness
in a world that curses dark-skinned
humanity, that catalogs what it calls
failures and that never once gave a
thought to those in the barrio who
prematurely die. I learned to weep with
words in a language my mother never
used to pray, in a part of town where
children asked about love while thinking
often of their last days. I have for much
too long wondered about this darkness?

THE RAIN

when it rains, I sit alone to
listen and watch birds whirl
above the streets in search
of shelter. when clouds weep,
I think of a story passed around
about the beginning of things and
imagine the sound of footsteps in
paradise. I see grains of sand in an
hour glass keeping time for each of
us, the way it slides to the jar bottom,
and the short distance it travels to a
last measure. I hear in the spaces between
raindrops gossip about love that speak
of the places that will always remember
us.

DREAM

I imagine the evening
arriving without a word,
unconcerned about the
languages living within
me, ready to take a seat
beside me to greet some
in the coffee shop with the
nervous dreams of faraway
lands. I am waiting for a
fresh night to spread her
wings and declare me a
lover who unravels thread
by thread the secrets of our
labored earth. you may even
imagine with me that tonight
sadness will clear up like leaves
on autumn trees and not a soul
will fear strangers in the city nor
dare deny the need to rearrange
the American dream.

LIFE TOGETHER

I returned to Bonhoeffer who told
us how to walk with a vulnerable
God, learn about what is going on
by finding love in the odd places
where judgement day is talked about
by the people at the edges who say
slavery has not ended. I have searched
for his revolutionary love to subvert the
laws of a butchering world, marched with
him whispering the gospel to me, held candles
to burn closer to heaven than to read church
creeds and entertained questions arising
from the experience of America's gallows
asking: does every human being truly have
lasting signs of divinity? I have come back
to Bonhoeffer's thoughts about a God who in
this world suffers, the way he joyfully served
a Crucified deity that did not let dread into
him and the tragic moment when Bonhoeffer
faced the criminals annihilating Jewish humanity
saying, "This is the end–for me the beginning
of life." I have reopened Bonhoeffer's pages to
confess with crucified people Good Friday does
finally save us.

THE WIDOWS

the world is more beautiful
in the morning when the old
ladies walk grandchildren to
school laughing like youngsters
with them. no one seeing them
fashions unkind thoughts and
the world is filled with the light
from the star that guides the poor
and the wealthy the same. when
I see them on that walk the day
is roomy and beneath the black
veils these widows wear you can
make out greying hair adorned
with beautiful flowers that make
them define everything with the
most treasurable simplicity. they
will spend time imagining partners
returning with a chunk of dragged
heaven to the block to kindly embrace
their imperfect lives and again hold
their wrinkled hands.

HOLDING HANDS

I was sitting on the stoop
watching the Puerto Rican
boys learning to dance salsa
from a gay Boricua who works
night clubs downtown in drag
who smiled at them and said not
half bad. sometimes, we talked
about the strange world in which
pious types like to judge others by
claiming the moral right to speak
using words not even in the Bible
or that ever came out of the mouth
of the theological renegade who was
nailed to a tree. on dance lesson
days, we became the many faces of
love, drifters from a Caribbean Island
in a barrio that unfolds sidewalks to
welcome men who hold hands and
girls who love each other. no one on
the block has forgotten what Angel,
also known as Angelita looked like
and the gracious way malicious gossip
was kicked to the gutter by him. no
one forgets to talk about the precious
moves learned from this drag queen who
was shoved into a language refusing to
understand by sanctimonious people
with callous hearts. on the block, we still
gather on the stoop to say Angelita was
beautiful and is now with Mathew Shepherd
and too many others taken too soon into the
manor in heaven.

THE LETTER

when I painted your name
on the building wall, shadows
warmed the alley, stars drew
close with earliest light and
I slipped into a dream that
could not wait for sleep. the
lovers with warm looks and
all their colors whispered to
me the words needed to find
each other sacred across the
border. like the tumbling birds
of the earth God fashioned, I
saw your beautiful Brown face
and tender lips say love is enough
for reminisced hours. though
nothing stays, I find you in the
spaces of my blinking eyes and
in the endless touch of your soft
hand.

CROSSING

this one took two months to
get here from the long journey
with a bag that had few changes
of clothing, pictures of family,
a grandmother's first communion
rosary and in zippered pockets
of the durable sack a small village
of packed dreams. she arrived
with the strain of border crossing
on her face, wanting to rest from
the more than three-thousand mile
trip, to forget the gangs that do not
spare kids, anxious to make her way
to the Catholic Church on Intervale
Avenue to light the candles for a
Sacred Mother and say thank you
prayers. she sat on the stoop that
night thinking about the adios waves
from those who said don't cry, recalled
floating across the river and making it
to this city in the North to begin a life
not hers. she sat with her memories on
the stoop, cried when no one was looking,
and again felt the men in uniforms who
held her against a rape tree with God just
watching.

THE MAYOR

we hardly remember the way you made
your way each Easter to Delancey Street
to bargain for a pair of pepper silk pants
and a rainbow Alpaca sweater like they
were items made of finest gold. we find
little time to recollect the rag tag Latin
rock band you started that had an English
name, the sound of your voice singing and
the big knife rumble on the block with the
jibaros fresh off the boat that did not like
being bedeviled by Nuyorican kids who
never looked back out of fear of being
turned into pillars of salt. sometimes, we
sit on the stoop thinking out loud that the
invisible hand of God that reached down
to grab you left a mark on the street where
you perished in the very city that erased
the day you were born. you lived doing
what you wanted, learning hard lessons
on the block, dropping out of school and
aware one day time would end. we have
not forgotten that you tagged the subways
with real names, with stories that revealed
what happened in school, church, home, the
streets and with the scribbles Keith Haring
one day exploited into white art. the storytellers
on the block each had a different point of view
though everyone misses you and hopes you are
cracking jokes with your maker the way you did
on the street that called you the mayor!

TOWN SQUARE

nobody told me I could not
show up in the town square
of the village of a tropical
island to find a once seen
uncle. it never occurred to
me that the place would be
colder than a winter block
and family would remain
distant like strangers. nobody
told me not to search every
corner of the island for home,
to find a place with smiles in
old San Juan listening to a
public television with American
shows playing for a tiny crowds'
ears in Spanish and wondering in
the odd hours of morning about
having been baptized in a colonial
religion in the basement of a Bronx
Catholic Church named after a Saint
who said Christ could not be found
in the chalice if not seen in the poor.
sometimes, I would stand on the banks
of the ocean at the edges of the shanty
town called La Perla with dope in my
blood saying God must be grieving in
heaven about the things we do down
here to creation.

NEAR

brother you should be here
this week feeling the Central
American breeze against your
brown skin, quietly desiring a
kiss from God, experiencing
faces smiling after civil war,
Mother Mary in the parks with
hungry street kids and Jesus
bending over to listen. brother,
you should be here to see night
lights, the sparkling mountain
sides, the elderly widows walking
the streets dressed with kindness,
the children playing in fields and
teaching us that God is not after
all a mute. brother, you should see
the entrance to the Cathedral that
holds Romero in her arms, in the
peace of the sanctuary where I sat
with campesinos who comforted
my weeping, in the candle I lit for
you at the altar and in the brown
hands of the mothers who worked
all day making tamales in the name
of the living and the dead. brother,
we talk about your Gethsemane and
feel you with us now looking into the
eyes of the infant in the nativity
scene made by Indian hands.

THE RUBBLE

I went to the block
and the building was
gone. in the rubble
beside two cans of
Ballantine Ale was
a pint bottle of cheap
wine. sweet memories
from the gone tenement
greeted me with hugs
and I made out in a pile
of shattered bricks the
faces of all the lost kids,
including Margarita who
walked with me to public
school. tonight, standing
by the empty lot I admit
my throat is knotted up
by the wasteland making
me shiver.

THE CRIMES

the committee of elected officials
spoke its final words after eighteen
months to tell the world what it knew
from eyesight. the news rushed across the
globe thicker than the dark waters of
the border river and there is nothing to
take as good news. while words pointed
to a solid way to deal with the man who
has yet to experience an honest day, we
are left pondering who will hand this
criminal a pass to place him beyond the
reach of law and assure the world that
clocks on these shores do not measure
time candidly.

WEDDING PHOTO

I have one photograph of my
father in a tuxedo with a long tail
rented on Southern Boulevard. he
is surrounded by family I never met
who are looking at the camera with
young undocumented faces beside
my mother who was a thirteen-year-old
Puerto Rican girl. the smiling faces in
the black and white picture represent the
beginning of an "I do" story that never
made the couple from different parts of
the Spanish speaking world a thing. I keep
the portrait on a shelf that holds many books
about the memory of God in order to reminisce
about the couple who never learned to stand any
closer together and ran faster from their children
than my brother when he was chased by the cops
at the train yard. sometimes, I look at that old photo
thinking quietly for a long time about the litany of
scars that young man and little girl carried across
borders, the color of their flesh that never lived up
to the white standard of America, their trembling
prayers for a better life and how I forgive every
one of their sins.

THE CHILL

when I dwelled on the streets
cold nights the stories of sin
and hell meant nothing to me
in the unkind hours. if you can
visit me in a nightly dream, see
the doors shut against my face,
feel the cold pavement beneath
your feet and chilling wind on
your face and even hear the demented
voices at prayer in the Hoe Avenue
church you would know a little bit
of the chill and lonesomeness that
knifed me. I lit candles in the waste
of an abandoned building that sheltered
me just ten blocks from the disorder
of a mother overlooked by a God she
adored. I slept under cardboard boxes
and sheets of newsprint hearing voices
from the street on occasion fading into
the room that still had linoleum on the
floor from a previous life. I can tell
you my heart thickened against God
who said nothing about the Spanglish
ghetto and though I am a long way from
cold nights they live in me like Psalms
of lament.

SLOWLY NORTH

they arrived at the place
many believed life begins
tired from weeks of travel,
no mothers around to hold
them, the hours moving along
without resistance in a place
eager to reject them. they came
with an entire world fenced
in their minds, questioning the
idea that God made this part
of creation with words and let
it spread in English. they fled
a place of nightmares carrying the
photos of the disappeared who
were treated like criminals for
being poor, memories of the police
competing to be supremely brutal,
hunger on the faces of thin kids
and days of lifting the dead bodies
of those quieted by gangs. they are
witnesses with Spanish tongues
whose stories will no doubt leave us
questioning the idea of God blessing
these United States, forever.

THE PANDAS

the seven-year-old seeing Pandas
with her very own eyes for the very
first time turned to look at her father
to say, "I don't think they're Zebras!"
the Panda looked up, the overcast sky
broke apart with laughter and sparrows
settling on the grass turned their tiny
heads. all the kids tried to talk to them,
a little English here and Spanish there,
but the two fluffy creatures could not
understand a single word. when it was
time to tuck the animals in for a night
of sweet rest the zoo visitors exited the
grounds more certain about the great
Poo mysteries disclosed by big bellied
Pandas from a faraway world.

THE DICTATOR

the tyrant is at his desk writing
a memoir that conjures stories
saturated with innocent memories
already enclosed by the flesh flies
gathered in the room to gorge on
the remains left in notebooks. the
man, who believes himself devout
though he has never read a divine
word in sacred parchments, neglects
to mention the poor that he pounded
into the earth and whose beating hearts
were like his made by God. the dictator
pauses before discharging more sinisterly
filtered words he will try to sell to the
church, ill-sorted memories telling
things significant to him that long after
he is gone will be rusted by truths
audaciously walking. there are clouds
above his roof full of tears for the lives
that never mattered gladly flooding his
wicked peace and tasteless confusion
of history with the freedom his days in
power left full of holes.

LAW

I dropped a quarter into a
a well of democracy all the
while wishing for the rule of
law to gush like a spring from
the pit to grab hold of white
politicians tightening chains
on the people excluded from
equality and lynched on old
Oak trees with the pledge of
allegiance recited at church
entrances entertaining onlooking
extremists with ghastly ideas
of belonging and freedom. now,
in democracy noisily declining
I see orange is the new white and
those who sport the color of the
times will never sing America is
my darker brothers and sisters. you
see a brand name face holds society
hostage to white crimes and a terror
wave God it appears cannot bring
down!

LAMENT

when my voice has no words
left, the wisdom of believing
no longer exists, the spot on
the stoop that belonged to me
is vacant and I no longer see
the moon, the stars, the clouds
or heavenly Angels who deliver
letters to the street, carry the barrio
with you and let the memory of
my voice sound loudly in the one
language between us wherever you
stand. when I come to the end
of a favorite hymn, the sparrows
sit on sickly trees with leaves not
yet shed, images of the crucified
carpenter on a cross rush into your
head, stand defiantly on the side of
life with prayer. when a Spanglish
word edges into space from my last
breath, weep with me for the broken
hearted scattered across this beloved
country who hate dark and sofrito
human beings.

YELLOW RIBBONS

in the Bronx I learned to
speak blanco without crossing
borders, having documents, or
uttering the pledge in broken
English. I shouted in art deco
corridor tenements in the last
hours of day about dreams knocking
on do not disturb doors of white
schools. we often sat on the stoop
counting worn out faces, with mothers
telling children to think American and
abuelas brooding about that day when
everyone from the old country and their
kids will be made. where I lived no one
felt ungrateful for salsa music, old country
stories, a quiet game of dominoes, a visit
to Crotona Park or tethering yellow
ribbons on fire escapes to welcome
Black and Brown soldiers back to
homes eager to listen to tales about
the hurt, the dead, the wretched poor
and old rich men's gains. where I
grew up the kids loved walking on
Southern Boulevard to stare at shop
windows and find winos with puckered
lips whistling tropical tunes and even
an occasional hymn. I lived on a street
where the bells of Zion promised justice
with old fashioned peace.

POLITICS

the history of modern politics in
the United States is the endless
gun violence in schools, a stormed
Capitol, a hard right conference in
the city where John F. Kennedy was
killed featuring a Hungarian president
decrying race-mixing to loud applause
like a 21st century Goebbels and stories
written in strewn drops of nonwhite
blood. the history of the government
that began when everything was young,
the land stolen, indigenous humanity
slaughtered, Black brothers and sisters
enslaved and women told to keep silent
is time exhausted by steps taken toward
freedom. the history of modern civics is the
memories of the vulnerable unheard, the failed
coup by the head of a crime family, the courts
looking away and the pages of the Constitution,
Declaration of Independence, the Bill of Rights
and Articles of Confederation deeply buried in
malodourous filth and far from biblical lessons
of love.

REDEMPTION

speak to me of redemption
said the old man damaged
by chaos in the barrio that
waits to see deities from at
least one religion come to pull
back the curtains hiding all
the healthy signs of life. some
days I believe nothing, tire of
dealing with the intolerable silence
of God and just when the sidewalk
flock of pigeons takes flight, I realize
with plain sense that no one around
here will slip into darkness.

THE PROJECTS

there is something about the
housing project brick walls
on Avenue D that require a
whole lot of mischief from
kids. in the ghostly light of
summer evenings they grab
spray paint cans giggling like
barefoot lovers leaving foot
prints on wet sand whenever
they write the stories of border
crossers or the names of those
caught by the river and in jails
praying San Oscar Romero Ora
Pro Nobis. down the very long
sidewalks in these monuments
to the luckless, the calligraphy
of the fatherless poor gallops to
the stone face of the buildings
in painted messages that scream
pay attention to the howling down
here.

PRAYER

for all the years of being told
there is power in prayer, the
time spent searching for the
right words to open the gate
to God's hiding place and the
days holding hands with the
working poor in inconspicuous
storefront houses of worship, I
have moved no more than an
inch closer to heaven. do not
mistake the questions in my heart
for darkness, I continue to say
my prayers yet never will agree
the mutilated world has a thing
to do with the divine will. today,
I pray to make sure every petition
made was heard and will be dearly
confirmed with a sign placed on the
road.

EXHALE

Nelly went to the bodega on
Intervale Avenue for .75 cents
worth of recao to season a meal.
She rushed skipping over cracks
on the sidewalk getting hold of
her shadow on the way back home
putting it in a paper bag. the shadow
was placed beneath her bed next to
a book titled, Meet Me in Paradise.
a whole new world began for Nelly
the day her shadow was packed in
a number 2 brown bag and hidden
under her bed where she imagined
in dreams the barrio inhabited by
people God adored. she opened her
eyes the next morning turned on the
light and the shadow was freed to enjoy
a game with her of hide and seek. after
playing, Nelly decided to sew the lively
friend back on to her beautiful Brown
skin.

TELLING STORIES

Tompkins Square Park in the
East Village has lived through
riotous communists, German
entertainment, hippie dreams,
punk music, drag shows, ranks
of migrant children waiting to
learn English at the local library
and Puerto Rican conga players
with breakdance kids. I loved to
sit on its uneven wood benches
with children on summer nights
telling them enchanting stories of
strange creatures only they could
see, tales from other worlds that
were undeniably scary, villages
where English was not spoken
and borders without Walls to keep
the poor from greater days. we often
trembled when ghosts from the last
year galloped through the park as a
little moon took its place above the
Lower East Side shouting in tongues
of lost things. we would wait for these
spirits to part then laughed loud enough
to guide Tito's blind abuelo to a park
bench.

STUBBORN

you who have left the world
prematurely rise with wings
above this thing passing for
life and flap them hard and
long until your gentle breeze
comes to us. watch over the dark
people who dream in the beautiful
black night when the weary bright
work day is done and over those
who have no memory of ever being
children. find us looking up at the
stars and let us know you will save
a place in the Lord's mansion for the
stubborn Spanglish hearts yearning
for holy love.

HERITAGE

Puerto Rico to me is the coqui
calling, congas at night, lovers
walking a sandy beach, preachers
reaching Boricua hearts, walks
down old village streets, sitting
beside a primeval waterfall and
a woman who gave me birth. I
can tell you too Guatemala is to
me the scenes my father loved,
rebellion against Spanish slavers,
criminal dictators, Uncle Sam killers
and love for the Indian blood pacing
through my veins shouting never give
up. what is it like to live in a world that
long ago delivered my mother and father
to a disenchanting country I call home?
perhaps, I will find a way to tell you after
a long walk on the dusty road once the way
to paradise.

AMERICAN RELIGION

we talked until the night spread over
the city about faith in America, then
Sofie shared her view that violence is
the religion of America and the gun its
Molech keeping people blind, deaf and
in permanent idol worship. she recalled
reading in school words now banned by
H. Rap Brown that explained violence is
equivalent to American apple pie. Sofie
went on to say citizens promote violence
on the internet and send fools into society
to go after each other with bales of hate for
people of color and the ghosts they invent.
for Sofie life is not arranged like pretty flowers,
God never sounds off and the law itself is a
way to break Black and Brown necks.

THE GRANDMOTHERS

I talked to a group of
abuelas this afternoon
saying kids cry in the barrio
about the suffering of the
poor. we sat for a couple
of hours discussing youth,
ghastly days of struggle, the
neighborhoods they live in,
broken dreams, the Spanish
forgotten and two birds on the
sidewalk that were dancing a
love story. they shared stories
of their homelands, splintered
days, years in the barrio and
dreams. I listened then dashed
to the Perez bodega returning
with flowers for them.

SINGING

I hear them harmonizing in
the tenement hallway in perfect
pitch better than the choir in the
decaying Presbyterian church, the
jingle of the Mister Softie truck
making rounds, the noisy laughter
wandering out of the little park
playground and tired songs about
white picket fences. I still hear
the sweet notes made, the Doo
Wop calls, the falsetto note and
those stubborn Spanglish tongues
never having to say they speak
a second language. these Boricua
boys made anthems for the weary
delivering them to a different light.
I mambo now and again these days
for no reason in odd places hearing
their songs erupting in me to point
out the wounded hope on all the city
streets.

THE BUS

I climbed in the trailway bus
at 41st street rode it through
the Lincoln Tunnel, down the
Jersey turnpike passing creeks,
farms, little towns, unknown
roads and heading West on the
highway to the state that grows
blue-eyed grass, morning glories,
poppies and daisies. I left at that
time when it is almost dark, the
city still asleep and people at the
station say nothing. on a front
seat in the bus a Mexican girl
with a white dress sat quietly
and ready for the three-day ride
to Los Angeles. once the trailway
rolled, sleep took over my thoughts
and the hours lived small mile after
mile. I dreamed this was my exodus
from the $3.75 cent room at the old
Hudson Hotel for junkies, winos and
homeless Puerto Rican kids. I pondered
how many lives can a fourteen-year-old
live, how many times can one ask God's
blessing and who the hell left this brochure
that Jesus Saves on the bus seat?

SHAMEFUL

the children naturally have no
say about the cold winter walks
to public school, the long lines
for a free meal, mothers leaving
for a 14-hour work day, kitchen
tables never covered with cloth,
the unforgiving city calling them
spics and why they descend daily
into unhallowed earth. the kids from
the block even now have no idea
of the way the rich downtown meet
to discuss in private parties how to
pick the skinny bones of the poor
right clean. these Brown boys and
girls cannot begin to imagine why
young women with babies in their
arms walked across two countries to
get away from war, gangs and femicide
only to end up hostages in a land pushing
white dreams. these children who kneel
with their mothers to pray cannot explain
why a Christian country knows too little
about being deceived.

HOBBY

when we were kids on the block
there was only one poor white
family living beside us that used the
word, hobby. the world our parents
fled that suffered poverty and saw
too many authoritarian slaughters
never used a word like hobby to
talk about what to do with spare
time. the strange new word left us
confused and speechless especially
having never heard such a term spoken
by elders who told stories about vultures
snacking on the dead. one afternoon,
following a very long and boring mass
that God missed, I left a bodega with
Papo wondering out loud if hobbies would
one day pay the hospital bills of the poor,
help mothers find decent work, keep brothers
and sisters from dying of AIDS, stop white
hate and save a rotten world. hobbies, I
thought belonged only to people who saw
us poor, illegal, junkies, thugs, and a threat to
a nation favoring death for those it calls
illegal spics.

THE LIBRARY

the library warms a spot on the block
and you can hear books calling from
its shelves and telling stories Spanish
speaking mothers have never read and
reciting poems in a language these
women struggle to speak. the books
sigh about love and blush with tales of
outlawed lovers talking in prohibited
tongues. there is no due date for the
voices leaping from pages thriving
in a Borges paradise, even those
banned across the country demand
attention, tonight. I stand in front of
the building having tears wiped away
by the words drifting from these precious
pages and then continue to stroll down
the block confessing in the beginning was
the word, waiting.

UNBORN

I came into the world
unborn, strolled down
streets without Spanish
names, born of a mother who
rode the subway too young,
never finished grade school,
and who carried a rosary to
mutter prayers. I traveled
with the missing, experienced
the nation that never spotted
Brown people like me and seen
days too dark for Adam and Eve
in paradise. fatigue does not worry
me and death does not frighten
me. I am glad not to give lip
service to original sin like so
many fellow citizens and prefer
to tell the truth about lynch land
for God's sake!

FEMICIDE

the young woman left her
hamlet for a city with a map
painted on the palm of her
hand, her long hair tied back,
a tiny suitcase with her worldly
things and an extra bag to keep her
most precious memories. she
walked long touched by a rush
of hope, drank water offered to
her along the way like it was
drawn from a well in the home
departed and took deep breaths
thinking about the inferno her left
behind sister would know. at night,
with shut eyes and leaning against
trees, she recalled images of femicide,
heard screams detonating in her head,
wept about disappeared girlfriends and
finally drifted into another time of
hardly risked sleep.

THE SOCIAL CLUB

we spent hours at the Ponce
social club on Home Street
leaning back on chairs next
to a pool table, the stench of
ale in the air tempting visitors
for a drink, Lefty behind the
bar on the telephone talking
to an uncle on the island about
a cousin laid to rest a week ago
in a Bronx cemetery. the social
club president staggered into
the room like a politician greeting
people by name and shaking hands
with the kids like they were made
of braille. no one in that space was
ever a suspect, we wore crosses on
gold chains and gave up cursing for
Lent like it mattered. members saw
seasons change yearly by looking out
the large tinted window installed by
Wilfredo's father, after he sobered
up from a rum-soaked night at the
Palladium with Machito and his
Afro-Cuban Orchestra. in time, the
Ponce Social Club faded away like
childhood though its memory has
not dimmed.

LA BODEGA

the little kids went to the
bodega to buy number 2
bags and 25-cents of peas
to shoot from straws like
particles of love at anything
that moved. they chased each
other on the cracked sidewalks,
running past the wall with
painted flowers, the mural with
family names, beneath the fire
escapes with dangling Puerto
Rican flags and Victor's father
who had his burnt orange 57
Chevy on milk crates to change
oil. today, these kids ruled the
street and raucously played in the
day giving them enough to make
life gorgeous. once back in their
apartments they kissed abuelitas,
forgot what hurts them and kneeled
to pray to a God who mattered.

SCHOOL

the week before the start of
school on the stoop with the
fractured steps where Lefty
wrote his name, the little kids
talked of the smell of sharpened
number 2 pencils, black and white
composition notebooks that spoke
English, Papo's mother who loved
leaning out the window on the first
day of classes to see kids heading
to P.S. 66 and abuelas who cooked
sopa de leche for breakfast. they
were excited the first days of learning
though not one of the kids liked being
told not to speak Spanish or spending
hours on the history of whiteness and
Black damnation. someday, they
thought the racist schools will use
woke books and the ghastly word spic
will hang in USA museums just like an
Arthur Smith painting of a lynching.

FLAG

I learned to pledge allegiance
to a flag full of stars flown on
the Navy ship my father sailed in
WWII to naturalize in the country
he learned to love. you cannot imagine
how often I twist my tongue in two
languages to swear about this nation
that finds thousands of ways to deny
equality to dark citizens. Maya said
some are dimly seen despite standing bold
on the other side of dull glass, nonetheless
people called spics like me are invisible
and nameless for pale citizens. in public
school assembly at pledge time, I rattled in
Spanish with friends about this land being
home and America a lifeless thing without
Black humanity and beautiful spics. in daily
schoolyard play, the Black and Brown kids
promised to march, explode and tongue lash
every drop of white washed story telling
attempted by teachers, while not forgetting
to murmur the old-fashioned forgiveness
taught by a lynched bastard who died in order
to save us with his precious dark life.

THE WINDOW

lights are still on in
the top floor apartment
where the woman who
observes the street from
her thin glass window
notices a group of boys
leaning on cars who are
passing around a bag with
a bottle of beer in it. a clear
moon glitters above the heads
of these Salvadoran boys who
know the names of more cities
in the USA than the land their
mothers fled. the woman who
watches them never breaks the
law, works seven days a week
to get paid four and still wants
a safer place to live. the boys on
the stoop smile when they see
her walking to the kind church
with undocumented kids. I sat
with this lady one evening at the
window noticing her beautiful
way of seeing Jesus keeping a
watch on things.

THE CRIMINAL

he keeps in a bedside table
the speeches of a Nazi who
made children drip with fear,
Jews beg for life and mothers
screaming at a voiceless God
while standing at the edge of
killing pits. no one ever imagined
the horrors of Auschwitz finding
a partner in the Oval Office, paraded
by the hate yammering of a twice
impeached president and storming
the Capitol on Three Kings Day. the
man in love with the speeches of a
butcher of Jews will one day learn you
cannot take wealth to eternity and the
hell named by migrant mothers, murdered
Jews and the victims of white supremacists
waits for him. those singing of heaven on
earth with terror filled eyes, people gassed
and despised believe blasphemous politicians
will find in Gehenna eternal reminders of those
they sentenced to short lives.

DARLING

pure love is spoken
by roses that slowly
open in your bedroom
disclosing kind mystery
and the scent of heaven.
you are perfume that
drifts across borders, light
that grandmothers hold in
la placita, the church bells
loudly ringing, the children
who laugh and infinity in
a kiss. day by day I have
lingered beside you while you
make history with ordinary
words, regard life worthy of
dreams and stored endless
joy inside of me. tonight, it
occurs to me that one day at
the end of life, time will not
agree it is finished and we will
find a way at the earth's last
stop to embrace like innocent
darlings.

THE BEGGAR

they never knew the beggar
who slept on the church steps
on Fifth Avenue covered with
plastic sheets and in clothing
stiff with year old filth. in the
echoing hours of night, he would
drink himself to sleep and not a
single intoxicated bone in his body
found the Lady of Guadalupe
on church grounds. once upon a
time he loved reading Whitman
and often recalled that the poet
claimed to know miracles though
most days the beggar never found
any walking the streets nor when
showing the hollow of his hand for
change. a stray dog that roamed about
at the woody end of Central Park often
came to him nightly putting light on
his sad face. you might say it was kind
of a miracle taking place on the sacred
ground where praying people never
asked for his name.

THE RIVER

life belongs to the river that
separates different worlds, it
belongs to the water that is
hope for some and a crime
scene for others. the river is
a place to feast before crossing
into the promised land, flowing
water God made to match the
sounds of freedom and dancing
relished by the formerly enslaved.
we travelled far with dreams for
the sake of the secrets held by the
ancient creek, to hold the hand of
Angels and cast the suffering from
disfigured skin. we talk to these waters,
holler at the Rio Grande, the souls lost
in the Sumpul River massacre, the kids
drenched with fear and gringos who can
not admit these waters set peasants
free.

COLORS

that Fall it was cold in the
east coast city, the trees in the
park were already changing colors,
the clocks were rushing toward the
last days of winter, people were draped
in abundant clothing and Miriam went
to the Cathedral to light candles for the
Holy Mother. the woman longed for days
with no more weeping or looking over her
shoulder and she sat in the sacred space,
thinking about all the señoras saying
prayers for distant villages and kids who
walk to school in them while belief in
God is decapitated by soldiers who take
orders signed by pens in blood. she left the pew
before completing another round of the
Rosary and walked back to the altar to set
aflame a fresh candle for asylum-seekers
put on buses and planes to satisfy the cruel
impulses of Red State governors who spend
time figuring out how to punish migrants
with made for television scenes.

THE CURTAIN

sometimes I feel like a cracked
glass blown down the sidewalk,
abandoned buildings on 3rd street,
the man on the block recalling the
days kids saw truth on the faces of
old women coming from Santero
meetings where nobody was ever
called spic. sometimes, I have a
deep-down feeling in my Brown
soul of giving up and tremble thinking
of the monsters waiting to pull a trigger
to welcome me to a grave. I even
occasionally hear abuelas muttering to
me about danger on the streets, spoiled
good news, the jagged edges of hope,
their reading of white hate and invitation
to find a little salvation in a poor lynched
man from Nazareth. sometimes, evenings
are thick when mothers make their way back
to the tenement from a day of hard labor in
a world reeking of crushed dreams.

PANHANDLER

you see him on the corner of
Tremont Street selling pencils,
air fresheners for cars and telling
stories dropped from the clouds
as you wait for the light to turn
green. you can hear him say God
bless you for handing over some
change and listen to him quickly
confess the good book lied about
the meek inheriting the earth. you
hear the Spanglish curses he throws
at the church that thinks beggars are
are not worth a damn thing. come
winter you will find him thawing in
the bathroom of the Simpson Street
subway stop, listening to the church
bells ringing in a yellow tower built
by immigrant hands, where an Irish
priest baptized him in the name of
the Trinity that forgets Puerto Rican
names. perhaps, some morning you
will hear Christ speaking through this
beggar holding out a hand for bread.

BIG STEEPLE CHURCH

for every visit you made
to the big steeple church
with the multimillion dollar
budget you were offered vile
stares and the crosses on the sanctuary
wall left you thinking of Brown kids
who left like Christ the world too
soon. you were never asked in the
pretty church to consider why chariots
swing low, Christ frees the enslaved
or why God is against racist preachers
blessing ropes for lynching trees. when
people like you appear in the worship
projected for learning a finer truth,
you have to walk to the altar rail with
centuries old chains. when you recite
the Lord's Prayer in the Spanish fellow
Christians in the pew discharge more
than a few choice words at you. sadly,
at the Lord's table people who show
up to find a white Jesus never admit
the messages Romero and Martin in
the name of Jesus spoke.

A FATHER'S DEATH

he will not return to answer
questions in bright light, to talk
of the heroin that took a son's
life, the bitter days living in the
land of fear, the burial hour in
which no one shed tears or the
sounds of mourning that did not
include him. he will never hear
the babbling laughter of the kids
never missed and nothing in his
world prepared the family in the
room holding foolish flowers for
his funeral.

THE FORGOTTEN

here we live at the edges of the
city leaving no footprints on the
sidewalks, yearning for the days
filled by sounds of Spanish in the
air, tree leaves singing in tropical
breezes, the early evening shouts
of children having a last round of
play and trying to use the warmth
of friends to find a way to make it
to the next dream in an ill mannered
world. how can I tell you about this
Golgotha, the longing for answers not
speaking in the light, the incessant
fright whispered by the undocumented
family in apartment 5C, or the sharp
stones the neighborhood grandmothers
carry as they wait for God to order them
to throw? how can I explain that every
morning we wake up worn out, bits of
nightmares still on the tip of our spic
tongues, unable to shake the feeling of
ruin and pleading with heaven to flood
us with signs?

THE CELEBRATION

this month you will not
celebrate with the Brown
people whose hands have
given your arrogant world
life. I know sitting on this
stoop with the Black and
Brown poor that white
America is not the product
of her own work. we know
too that the Columbus Day
you plan to celebrate when
Hispanic Heritage month ends
is tribute to a Western killer,
human trafficker and grand
wizard of Christian violence
and rape. why not ask the people
weary of torture and death about
the centuries of white crime that
make the dark-skinned savior from
Nazareth weep.

THE MOON

the moon is relief by the hour
from all suffocating politics,
an antidote for poisonous hate,
a medical prescription for lovers
and a healthy nightly dose needed
by people condemned to live with
bad dreams. when you cannot sleep
it waits for you in the night sky like
a good luck charm, it teases you with
silvery light and guides you through
the mysteries known by elders. the moon
is a favorite thing by those sitting silently
in darkness and a rock whose light the
wind gently pushes across fields. as the
years turn on this moving earth, the moon
shines everywhere on the going tides and
leans toward hearts in wonder and before
the night is done and two spoons of it are
drunk, the moon lets us have a great big
swallow beneath the old crooked tree of
love.

THE OTHER SIDE

you are on the other side of
the border, the land that is a
parish for God, home to exiled
fathers and the only place left
to visit a church to hear about
the history of the still born life
of your country. you stand beside
the wall flinging your arms to
heaven, near dead from poverty,
weeping for the world you are
to leave, the villages older than
America you may never see, the
unbearable fear that family will
bear and imagining already the
cracks in your dreams on the far
side of the boundary. you stand
on the Spanish speaking side of
the artificial line sketching in the
dirt truth recipes that you will try
to live and telling a short story of
the hope you bring to a new world
of darkness that has not yet started
to scratch heaven.

SIMPLE

the simple things are bound
to happen unexpectedly like
smiling at night that still shows
up, listening to the Supremes
on an outdated cassette player
beside the old man who sits on
the corner spit shining shoes,
entering the church to light a
candle for the Saints that have
still not come to wipe faces of
tears, walking into the apartment
with crosses in a bedroom, pictures
framed and hanging on walls with
the faces of a family that rise every
morning refreshed by the sound of
Spanish and still finding time to rejoice
about the charms of life and simple
love. the simple things are full of
surprises like mothers comforting sick
children with ancient lullabies and God
showing up on the block to answer
questions the poor have been asking
since the Word became flesh among
the damned and deprived.

THE PRAYERS

after leaving church without
answers, I saw the book of prayer
on the stoop written on the faces
of the Puerto Rican kids cracking
jokes. they dropped Spanglish words
God wanted translated. they yelled
bendición to people lately invited to
the Last Supper, disenchanted mothers,
halleluiah pietists and skeptics in the
alley knocking down a bottle of Midnight
Express. they begged the great dodger
in heaven to keep them in school,
make sure white bosses paid tired
workers, and to let them harvest a little
bit of Boricua truth in the public school
history class that never features them.
they talked about the church crowded
once a week with people showing up
to pray about the things, they hardly ever
think about during work, then Tito jumps
into the conversation to tell friends to take
number 2 pencils to Mrs. Novi's math class
to conjure equations that might help them
make a rewarding grade.

SER OR NOT TO BE

I was not surprised by the leaps
of imagination taken by the public
school kids rehearsing lines from
Shakespeare translated into their
Spanglish tongue, you know, ser
or not to ser is la pregunta. they
knew the middle school Hamlet
lesson of friendship, madness,
religion, politics, and revenge too
well for it played daily in the cross
winds of the block and most times
after school when they came up for
air far from the chemistry of whiteness
in their Caliban world. These precious
brown boys and girls from P.S. 118
were glimpses of hope in mothers'
misty eyes and here they sat with
topical lessons that would surely
make Shakespeare drift to Europe
and back to the cracked steps of
buildings in the Bronx. these kids
living in the shadow of the world
hint the divine truth residing in the
barrio in plain view.

MURMURS

on the radio there is a company
running adds that offer to teach
Spanish the fast and easy way so
you can order a reggaeton dish
in Puerto Rico, look at a world
of things not made in English
and talk beneath stars to people
in colonial towns living with the
history sanitized in books. I should
sign up for American English lessons
myself to better understand the kids
leaving schools who reject nonwhite
authors' observations. nope, I am
just kidding about paying to learn a
language that disapproves of people
without pale skin and I agree with the
the block critics who think it's not
worth paying a ton of money to learn
a babble of shit!

TECATO

the junkie living in the park
by the East River spent the
morning reading logos on
planes flying across rooftops
to La Guardia airport. he had
been living off borrowed time
for more than a decade collected
from a white therapist at Harlem
General Hospital after a first visit
to kick a jones. Motown songs
flowed in his veins and a horde
of vultures mysteriously waited for
him to end life with an OD. he wore
the face of every tecato on the block
and smug church goers believed Jesus
could not even save him by hanging on
a tree. after the counting, he recalled
the Rikers Island prison library where
he read a few lines from the Nuyorican
poets who wrote in the perfect broken
English that made him tremble about
the idea in their written words of a new
American me.

WINOS

he wore the thrift shop coat
picked up at the church where
years ago he was baptized by
an Irish priest who spoke in
Spanish. he looked warmer
than the guys huddling in the
television room on the detox
floor of Beth Israel Hospital who
straight or high could never find
peace. he headed toward the sweet
sound of laughter coming from the
laundromat on the corner where the
bus arriving from Manhattan after
a run through the weariest streets
of the Bronx made its last stop. the
winos were cracking jokes, some
danced to the sounds of the washing
machines in the room, others cursed
the hungry years and Mr. Coat pulled
out a pint of wine smiled at his nick
named friends and then sang a line
from a hymn that went Nearer My
God to Thee. he took a sip from the
pint bottle, passed it to Hank and
launched into a Spanglish soliloquy
about the barrio holding back tears
and throwing in a few jokes to make
drunkards smile.

WALTON AVENUE

how love is lived on Walton Avenue
came up the day you saw featherless
head pigeons hopping in front of the
bodega. you wanted them to shout
your name flying above little Ana's
head, while dropping the last rustling
leaves from Crotona Park on the two
of you embraced. you never imagined
your beating heart with all its yearning
would stop one odd hour nor that sacred
life would bolt. you did not leave before
saying love is every song in paradise, a
kind day on the street and the sweetest
faith worn for clothing. my dear Mayor
of Walton Avenue people around here say
you are worth the full weight of heaven in
tears.

SNOW

the street was blanketed in snow,
sounds were muted, the wind
pushed us over the sidewalk, an
old woman was waving her arms
by a window and for the cold night
nothing was better than a good pair
of boots. the street lamps along the
avenue offered quiet light while a
few more snowflakes made their way
to land on our heads and some stuck
to the icicles dangling from a windowsill
of Cuca's apartment who was behind
with her life. a few Puerto Rican boys
shoveled snow for the owner of the
corner barbershop. as always, city
snowplows left a huge mound of snow
in front of building 1203 where the
Jewish watch fixer who loved snowball
games with kids lived. we played with
him snowy days yelling broken English
and hearing him yell back to us in Yiddish
ways.

THE REFUGE

we loitered in the hallways
of old tenements with colored
tile in the Bronx one by one
proposing a song in the one place
believed perfect. we unpacked
history in a corridor that had
been without light for a very long
time, not making any excuses for
the white adults who came around
the block to find a little mystery by
studying us just to say in the pages
of books gathering library dust these
kids are old for their young years. we
sang harmonies like the Four Tops
waiting for mothers to come home
from back breaking work, then kneeling
with them in front of altars to Jesus
where they wept about how they could
not afford to feed their kids. we sang for
hours untouched in those tenement halls
by the steady pounding from the world
detesting us.

THE TREE

there is one tree on this street
and every year it tells us in plain
sight Fall is here. its brown leaves
drop to the sidewalk, they are lifted
by the wind, whistled up the side
of tenements and left to rest on
the stoop like a thing of ageless
beauty quietly waiting for dusk. I
have often thought prayer is made
of this kind of thing filled with secrets
nature long ago began.

THE ANTHEM

in a country with white supremacists,
centuries of slavery doing evil like
Judas counted change, the victims of
American history list their seasons
of rage. truthfully, yellow ribbons
are never tied on old Oak trees, instead
Black and Brown bodies are dangled
from them in front of court houses and
churches that adore a savage God. the contract
historians deny avoid this sickening history
but the dead live on in the suffering of
tangled hearts. in a country that wants
to make us disappear by teaching stories
of an innocent history that overlooks the
the slave owning anthem writer Francis who
praised the home of the free and lashes
for the enslaved you can be certain dawn's
early light will deport every fabricator that
pretended innocence to spaces exclusively
deserved.

LOVE SONG

I cannot tell you why little
things nourished hearts in
the neighborhood with spray
paint messages on the tenement
walls. things like admitting love
is Lela holding her new born on
the stoop rushing headlong into
single motherhood or bread from
Valencia Bakery shared by famished
people dropping kindness on the
the streets or kids after school who
dash up steps to apartments faster
than Moses ascended Mount Sinai
to hug abuelas. these simple things
press us into moments of love with
a longing for the impossible dreams
older than time on earth.

SORROWS

what more can we say
about this intolerant land,
the people who build walls
around them, the baseless
fears inhabiting them, the
many ways they try to hold
dark humanity responsible for
national demise and countless
sanctimonious mouths reciting
small prayers. how many years
must be spent staggering for work,
a good school for US born kids,
a decent place to live, doctors
who care to treat patients in
Spanish or cursing the news
that gets foreign names wrong?
even now we cannot say what
morning brings, when la migra
will sweep us up at work, when
godly light will fill our fright or
the exact time the terrors of this
nation's hate will stop lashing us
with rods. when will the Cathedrals
condemn the language God forbids
and draw open the curtains that keep
making life too dark?

ESSEX STREET

I walked to Essex Street market
where once you could enter the
corner Jewish candy store and
ask for a chocolate egg cream
for just fifty-cents and wonder
why there was no trace of egg
in the drink. history has now
given the old market a new face
with freshly planted trees on the
sidewalks, Spanglish, and Yiddish
making appearances in old photos
adorning walls in chic cafés, where
a few shots feature Puerto Rican kids
fond of making scooters from the
wheels of tossed skates, two-by-four
wood and Perez bodega milk crates
decked with improvised handle
bars. I made one of them powered
it with pure bean protein that white
midwestern college kids referred to
as health food—go figure! I sat quietly
for a couple of hours on Essex Street
with two friends who refused to work
on Yom Kippur and shared memories
of mischievous child's play with me taking
a sip of coffee after each tale.

GUNS

guns make their daily rounds
leaving shell casings next to
bloody pools remaining from
children wanting only to read
books with wide eyes. guns are
like American apple pie, unending
devotion, an unquestioned God, a
loaded menace, killers venerated
by right wing history, instruments
of hate and endless reticence about
crimes. guns shoot angels in heaven,
satiate the world with prayers, and
churches with milk and cookies, while
the innocent receive slugs. guns put cracks
in comely church bells, open passages
to hell, permission for violence and endless
disregard for the vulnerable removed by the
wicked in the world. guns, a modern-day
Molech, an idol of death, cruelty, sorrow,
and screams of the terrified. guns, the latest
version of a lynching scaffold where devils
slaughter the innocent.

PUBLIC HOSPITAL

the day I was born, there
was mystery in the city
hospital, yelling in the
corridors, mothers' eyes
lighting up, gladness on a
student doctor's face and
a priest making rounds with
evocative prayers. Papo
was born on the same day,
the last winter snow fell then
on the South Bronx earth
looking like a page from a
Dickens story capable of uniting
heaven and earth. with infants
in their arms mothers returned
to the block full of dreams and
ready to let the future happen,
eager to kneel in front of altars
in their bedrooms to say appetizing
prayers to the God that watched
over them and these kids on the
streets.

THE BENCH

after climbing out of a hole
in the sidewalk and rolling
passed the front entrance to
the police Precinct called Fort
Apache, he took a seat on a park
bench next to the homeless in
tents. on the crippled block that
is never talked about in dinner
parties where Martin and Chavez
are simply recollected dead, he
opened a container with miracle
rice from the Boricua restaurant
up the street and smiled at the little
kids emerging from their canvas
homes with the backpacks donated
by the local Catholic church. the
kids were ready for a new day in
school made for them to gossip in
Spanglish about lessons that make
them flinch. he looked around the
little park, thought about the great
wealthy city with leaders who talked
about salvation for the white chosen and
laughed at such theologically misguided
stupidity.

AWAKE

slowly the morning awakes
and a breeze exquisitely comes
to me. I watch the day get up
unconditionally and with deep
affection for the rabbit emerging
from a light haze and rushing to
that place on the other side of the
street it believes a home of infinite
space. in this dazzling time all
theology cannot near the magnificent
experience of wakefulness that these
speechless moments offer.

ROOF CAFÉ

I love the corner counter in
the café with a view above the
roof-tops of the city, the sight
of a crowded street like a painting
in the modern art museum, and
momentary cheer inside a glass
of house brew. I am gripped by
two men in three-piece suits in
a game of chess and the poor old
man on the avenue holding a sign
inviting charity from pedestrians.
the sun shines a little spot of light on
the spoon at the edge of the table and
I think it nature giving the café a wink.
I take a last sip of coffee and wave so
long to the Ukrainian waitress who has
lived for years on the Lower East Side
a few blocks away from the street named
for a poet from her old country, Taras
Shevchenko Place.

GUN LOVE

every day beyond the attention
of the news shows a school bus
load of children and another of
adults who have done no harm
is killed by gun violence. daily
the thoughts and prayers spoken
never make it all the way to heaven
and are the nonsense said by those
who would not walk a mile with Jesus
gun less. there are already too many
places holding the memory of our
beloved dead and the bullets that
rocket within earshot are always
chilling. fear, hate, ethnic cleansing,
slaughter, revenge dance on the tip
of fingers that pull triggers to make
lives end and the NRA says after each
terror show God blesses guns. every
day the brokenhearted stoop over graves
in a society praising violence more than
it recalls the innocent dead and families
weeping about those damn thoughts and
prayers assaulting them.

THE FUNERAL

the people saying property cost
goes down when Black and Brown
humanity moves in are too full of
delusional whiteness to admit the
value of the nation has taken a major
hit with a bonfire of delusions expelled
by the democide man and repugnant
members of his Klan. Whitman heard
America singing in mechanics, carpenters,
masons, mothers, shoemakers, and many
others but these days I see America home
to guns, freedom for some, lynching by
people settled on stolen land, in places
built by slave hands, territories savaged by
manifest destiny and all blessed in the name
of white supremacy. the white arrogance goes
out of its way in houses of worship to trample
King's dream, the wealthy do Columbus size
crimes and dark-skinned people persistently
wronged pass their mourning from generation
to generation. turning away dear Whitman from
Victorian sentimentality, the Captain I fear is not
only fallen but, in the present funeral march of
America near cold dead!

BEAUTIFUL

you asked for a thing of beauty
in coming evening, the passing
loveliness that you promise for
an eternity to keep, an image for
all your sweetest dreams that will
guide you into salacious light and
that touch of magic that smooths
the cracks in the sidewalk that trip
you. the journeys you have made
at the edges of life, the numerous
times you gave thanks to live with
the mysterious charms in this half
full world, the abundant stillness
of your unrewarded search for a
God too quiet and the delicate way
that you tilt your head in prayer I
must tell you sing to me about what
not to miss when searching for beautiful
things.

THE HOLY

we laid an offering of roses
at the feet of Mother Mary,
the brown-skinned girl, who
no one doubted found ways
to hear the words spoken to
her by those with breakable
lives. the sanctuary that held
us was breaking with the light
of candles that stirred visions
for people waiting for the sacred
mother's breath to be their very
own. on this side of the dark river
where you never smell dew on the
sidewalks, where children wake up
hungry for school, mothers who only
speak Spanish are daily signs of hard
work and the old 7-Eleven around the
corner is packed with truckloads of
young men looking for work, you sacred
Morenita speak to us from Spanglish
painted alley walls. we are not invisible
to you, far from your voice nor alone
protesting the wicked in this crucifying
world.

CATECHISM

they let us out of school early
once a week to attend on Hoe
Avenue catechism instruction
in the office of an Irish priest
who spoke better Spanish than
the neighborhood kids. that was
the day I discovered English can
express itself on occasion without
turning its back on God and even
describe the metaphysics the bunch
of us in religious instruction exhaled
daily. the priest who was the son of
Irish immigrants entertained us in his
office with an accordion that made us
curiously listen to the instrument alien
to our Boricua world. I recall excited
conversations on the way to the church
office, faces full of suspicion, jokes about
a Spanish speaking God being late and
wondering if redemption and the merciful
Christ would come to the block once we
learned the catechism required by the church
keeping the Puerto Ricans in the basement
for Sunday worship.

MASONS

the masons who built Mexico
put up scaffolding in front of
the old building on third avenue.
they carefully tested the wood
planks holding workers. Hector
lugged bricks and mortar in a
wheelbarrow, thinking of the
lips across the border he has not
kissed for more than a year and
how talking about life with rapid
fire Spanish is like spitting nails
melded with good old cross the
border grace. these workers
showed up in the city with actual
human dreams and they have been
fixing broken buildings in Spanish
Harlem with injured tongues that
make them stutter more than Moses.
imagine, these bricks freshen up
old buildings for sale to café latte
lovers who trash the dreams of these
Mexican masons at least a thousand
times a day.

TRANSISTOR RADIO

one day of an innocent year,
I left to live miles away in an
abandoned tenement though
longing for the sound of Radio
Wado in Mother's kitchen on
school mornings. I still hear
the salsa tunes that poured out
from the transistor radio resting
on top of a dingy refrigerator
below a black kit-cat clock with
moving eyes and tail. I feel the
rare gentle caress of a hand that
reminds me of living in Spanglish
America, experience fond points
of memory with siblings smiling
in a single-mother home and return
to the long walks to a Junior High
School whose commencement year
I never saw. I admit being haunted
by dark Bronx shadows where pieces
of my Boricua soul remain, with big
walls around it to keep me from dying
like a blind man who never saw stars at
night. You know, I have been an outcast
longer than a speaker of English in this
prison house that cannot keep me from
calling this land home!

BUS RIDE

the bus left the Times Square Station
early Tuesday, light was beginning to
break on the city, cars were lining up
at the Lincoln Tunnel preparing to cough
beneath the Hudson River to cross into
Manhattan for daily work, the mother
sitting next to me told her child in perfect
Spanish Los Angeles was several days far
and I was lost in thoughts about a future
coming toward me. I watched the driver pull
on the steering wheel, after a few minutes,
turned to see behind me and noticed there
were empty seats scattered about the cabin
waiting no doubt for witnesses to board at
the next stop for the long trip to the West
Coast with riders exhaling stories of escape.
I cracked open the tinted window to let
out words along with laughter, fell asleep
on a long stretch of the Jersey turnpike
and woke at a filling station where the
bus stood with thirst.

FAITH

when my eyes opened in the
darkest part of early morning,
the moon a silvery disk, a dog
finding its way on the sidewalk
with muffled barking, flowers
still retreating from the coming
winter, I could see the precious
pageantry of mystery and taken
for granted wonders easing into
the new day. when I woke to the
questions of the world outside so
gently asking I dared to believe that
war can become peace, the ladders
leaning on the tenement walls lead
to heaven, hate can be forgotten by
love and light will shine once again
in earth-shattering darkness.

ORTIZ FUNERAL HOME

the funeral home with the
Spanish name has been on
the corner of first Avenue
ever since the projects four
blocks over became a Puerto
Rican haven. I saw it for the
first time before learning to
speak English and praying like
it mattered for the poor. I walked
by the place never seeing the
Ortiz family who owned the
business, or smelling death
exiting its front door. I can
tell you the scent of flowers
delivered to its steps was in
the air most days. I have been
in the reception rooms of the
funeral home too often, sat with
others folding sadness in their
souls more than once, searched
the memorial spaces for signs of
God, rehearsed tragedies with
teens in Spanglish and madly
wept about the familiarity with
death wrapping Black and Brown
hearts in that place.

RIO GRANDE

I sit by the water of the Rio
Grande reading it for signs
of history, stuffed memories
from the Brown side of the
world, the stories of Spanish
speaking people who left old
Cathedrals with lives too far
from God. I see messages on
floating pieces of wood drifting
north with the images of Saints
carefully sketched by trembling
dark hands. I hear the steps of
wet shoes behind me, voices of
two women with a small child
saying America will be against
them, and turning my head I see
a thirteen-year-old girl, dipping
her hand gently into that of her
mother, who with a faint smile
on her angelic face said but we
are not against them. they share
a little laughter and walk out of
sight into the darkness protecting
them.

THANKSGIVING

here the children sit in
the tiny kitchen of the
apartment with pernil or
like the Irish family on
the first floor like to say
pork shoulder. they are
about to lift their hands
toward the ceiling that hides
heaven on the other side of
the fifth-floor roof. they ask
in New York City's precious
Spanglish for blessings to rain
on thanksgiving and the little
things they cherish. they have
prayed, laughed, and suffered
at that kitchen table like in the
beginning of things when sweet
bites offered life.

DOPE

they say the junkie kids on
the block have left aside the
stories in the church, the old
traditions their abuelas have
invoked to conjure divine spirits
they think live in special words
that inhabit us. I have roamed
the alleys with them, made fires
in trash cans that conversed with
their thin shivering bodies on the
corner, wept with them in a world
that treats them like criminals and
passed around tales of families that
abandoned them to needles. these
strung out kids would like to hear
priests name the sins of the world,
why they live terrifying days, the
reasons they are not missed in school
and who cares that one-by-one they
perish.

THE PASSAGE

I dreamed of a dog barking
at waves rolling in from the
ocean on a tropical beach,
the passage of time on earth
obvious beneath her sinking
paws, with a wall of doors on
the horizon each one left open
to hide nothing and a group of
Spanish speaking kids building
castles with sand while the sun
traveled West. I dreamed the dog
came over to me begging for bread
with words it had picked up from
people and I saw a blind elderly
widow reaching out to touch the
faces of the children at play with
a wrinkled hand that made me smile
big.

THE RUINS

you can feel this hotel close
to the ruins near where roosters
crow to wake the sun that rushes
rooms each morning. this inn
emerged from the ashes of a civil
war and on the edges of the city it
shares stories that otherwise would be
left silent. in the clumsy hours, when
love disappeared on village streets,
in the fields, valleys, and mountains,
just when peasants invaded churches
in search of a Crucified God and wind
chased newspapers down wicked alleys,
the poor asked their Savior to let the
brokenhearted experience the life soldiers
wanted to end. you can still see painted
messages on walls for heaven on these
streets not long ago flattened by government
sponsored criminals.

WAITING

in this time of waiting
for a border crossing God
to become flesh in the stench
of a stable, I find myself with
hungry kids on church steps
sharing troubles. I talk with
them about their thirst for
simple love, imagining long
journeys to the East guided
by a star, kneeling before the
manger and turning away from
self-righteous Christians that
cannot see Bethlehem sings of
peace on earth for the poor. with
kids in the ramshackle tenements,
sleeping under newspapers, curling
up in box houses, rejected by family
and even baptizing priests, I sit on
church steps to wait for Christ to
cry like an infant for them.

PROTEST

why do I question the silence
of God on these streets? I
suppose it has to do with the
blood stains on sidewalks, in
the apartments, the rooftops,
jailers' prisons, and the places
Jesus himself and pious people
do not step out to see. we have
learned in the barrio to speak to
God with the same language of
grief living in us in spaces that
widen with the perpetual absence
of good news. why do I complain
about God? perhaps, it is just my
inelegant way of reaching for salvation
and shouting from the slums about
sorrow yearning to finally see a
divine sign.

THE STAR MATTERS

the tenement windows are robed
with lights and sprayed snow

by the Puerto Rican mothers
waiting with trusting prayers

for the morning when the clocks
strike Christmas. they light glass

candles in bedroom altars adorned
by the images of Saints and Mother

Mary to whom they promise never to
give up even when they are out of work

and overcome with fear. beside a
simple bed Carmen in apartment

5C keeps the good book that is full
of magnificent secrets offered for

pain very close to her on those nights
wide awake. the kids who live with

her stand nightly by the window
looking at the sky trying to find

San Nicolas floating on clouds and
whispering in Spanglish until the

last cotton ball cloud drifts away and
shadows chase light across the alley

to the boulevard. when there is only
silence, the kids rush to their mother's

side where hope cannot be vanquished
nor darkness overcome light.

THE MEANTIME

when we sat on the building
steps listening to Symphony
Sid on a transistor radio play
the latest Salsa music, older
men and women on the block
were in their mid-twenties and
we thought our teen mothers who
hustled petty wages to feed us, clothe
us and keep a roof above our skinny
heads were grown women. we talked
for hours about Orchard Beach like it
was just another piece of Puerto Rico's
ocean, the BX 12 diasporican bus load
headed to the Boricua Riviera with people
happy to have new lives in New York
City and plenty of dreams to fill public
libraries. we have grown older talking of
how life in the barrio is based on other
people's decisions including Joey's O.D.
on a roof on Intervale Avenue from dope
delivered to the slums by Uncle Sam's
Viet Nam vets. we have passed the years
observing the hate America dresses with
flags, crosses and screams.

BEAUTY SCHOOL

Sunday morning the sidewalk
was lined with flowers for the girl

who came from an island village
in a Caribbean Sea with one bag

and two years of schooling. with
her came stories of crooked church

leaders and the conspicuous tales
of colonial landgrabs that pushed

her to victimizer's shores. that
evening, when the music played

on the streets to celebrate Carmen's
completion of study at the Paris

school of Cosmetology the stars
wept in heaven to tell afterlife

subjects about Carmen. she wore
a small gold cross around her neck,

held a child by the hand and sat on
stoop giggling like a little girl washed

clean by Yemaja, the Goddess of the
sea and comforter of African slaves.

with her new barbers license in hand
Carmen retreated the block party to her

single-room apartment imagining better days to come.

SCHOOL BOY

you can hear singing pouring
out of the Pentecostal storefront,
notes dancing down the sidewalk,
playing for crying mothers left
alone by men who never said their
names on the block. they gather
with sad eye kids who have a long
list of step-fathers who came and
went like unexpected rainfall. the
old women in the church once teen
girls learning English believe they
must keep watch at night and that
explains why they cannot find
sleep. one Puerto Rican boy rushed
home today to share stories from
religious instruction class about
camel's squeezing through the eye
of a needle. he wanted to turn the
old priest's words into a clumsy
prayer and ask why Jesus who left
an empty tomb did little for the poor
like him? staring into a bowl of arroz
con leche, the seventh grade boy made
up a prayer of invitation for Jesus thinking
he might show up.

ADESTE FIDELES

the dogs in the alley bark
in the long night without
motive, across the broken
sidewalk the curious about
politics talk in a warm corner
of Gordo's grocery store and
observe a backroom with an
altar with candles burning. Papo
reminds them last year it was so
cold the pipes in the building froze
and the super walked the boiler
room holding a torch to them unable
to keep back laughter thinking hell
for Boricuas is a New York winter.
the conversation turned to matters
of life in transit, the realization that
home was elsewhere and questions
about it on the sharp tongues of the
Spanglish speaking kids then written
on walls. the fire escapes outside had
ice formed on them reflecting the
light from a streetlight patched with
flyers unreadable like a vacant church.
eyes fell on Wilfredo who suddenly
talked about the Midnight Mass for
Christmas, whether they could show
up a little drunk to scream in the very
middle of it—Adeste Fideles! Venite,
Adoremus! Venite Adoremus, dominum!

DIGITAL TRADE CARDS

the narcist has minted digital
trade cards that show him in
photoshop heroes garb. the
unrepentant fool cannot hear
the world is laughing and truth
will remain his dreadful fall. this
man with little good to show limps
for a $99 dollar lie with a brand
new money-grubbing scheme. the
global idiot believes he is on top
of the clouds but truth be told there
is not a patch of land anywhere on
earth that weeps for him. the grifter
makes a sales pitch mostly to his
bamboozled fools who love dancing
on stages of delusion and with this
former guy's high achieving bullshit!
what will come next to occupy the
the mind of the country club asshole
selling digital trading cards? surely,
this waking crime wave with white
supremacist fancies is the least wanted
superhero ever pitched.

AFTER

tonight, the star is invisible to
the eye and shepherds gently
speak with the hungry, the homeless,
the broken, the loathed, the lost and
humanity in need. after a day of
sharing gifts you can hear whispers
saying is that all there is to the Christmas
feast? the silence tells us there is more
and after meeting the infant, we pray not
to walk away from the manger disobedient
servants. today, remembering the stable,
we dare leap into the hours of a coming
New Year and with trembling lips ask
you dear Word made flesh to lead us away
from temptation for the sake of the sublime
star that guided the poor and broken however
slowly to you. today, we will light candles
in the Cathedral of a martyr to confess God
will let the nations have their hate but love
will triumph like the promise of streams to
come in the desert.

THE WAIT

at the bus stop the faces
look thin. they wait for the
late driver conjuring the
battles experienced long ago
on village streets. the haunting
comes like a hanging day after
Sunday.

THE SEASON

today, Jesus is carried in Maria's
arms across the border where
buzzards circle the air. she just
walked away from the place the
narcotraficantes pocket dollars
thanks to unsighted Uncle Sam, the
land where policemen carry M16
rifles to open wounds in villages
and snuff the life of the poor who
were once Spanish property. they
come from the land the Department
of State warns its citizens not to visit,
a part of the world no one considers
human, a region where the dead speak
of Christians killing Christians just like
in Europe and the States. they have
traveled a long way just to speak in
broken English followed by assassins,
to write the names of peasants on Walls
sullied by USA crimes and pounded by
the hypocrisy of freedom. perhaps, after
this crossing the blameless child in Maria's
arms will not be killed at the margins like
Christ!

MYSTERY

sometimes, looking into your
eyes I see the mountains caught
up in pure truth and it makes me
feel delirious. sometimes, when
night offers us a sky full of stars,
heaven takes me by your hand and
every outdated idea of the divine
is tossed into the East River and the
magic of love enters the ordinary
world. sometimes, when I caress
your hair the tearful world has a
moment to live happily and paradise
issues forth in history. sometimes,
your lips share the work of justice
in places unknown even to the sacred
scriptures flattered in churches and I
say then that exile will never be too
sad.

THE CONVERSATION

despite dogged time aging
us, we come back to the block
to bid each year farewell, to see
a trio of Jehovah Witnesses enter
tenements in search of souls, to
talk about the Pentecostal storefront
yelling hallelujah like hard truth and
the Catholic church on the corner there
in the same spot changing faces for more
than 100 years. newspapers are pushed by
gusts of wind to our feet with headlines rarely
shaking the world to consciousness and always
useful bedding on the split sidewalk for nostalgic
Puerto Rican winos. we stopped believing speaking
english brings clarity, perfect happiness, or anything
resembling good thinking. there is more than enough
light in Spanglish to lead us away from the dark and
the cruelties entertained by the backsliding churches
pretending God is not ashamed of them. we watched
a solitary pigeon in flight settle on a fire escape and
tossing out a few more sentences with our new world
tongues wondered if God still had any well-meaning
plan for the people dragged in the world by the hair
that heaven apparently forgot.

THE HYPHEN

I live on the hyphen
with whole worlds on
either side, caressed by
shadows in the odd hours
of each day, listening with a
few to the shouts of border crossing
people and satisfied with the sweet
reality of simply calling this place
home. I imagine once more the
names we cling to between and
betwixt, recalling graffiti on a wall
just before the spot where the subway
goes back into a tunnel that says Oscar
Romero Ora Pro Nobis, smiling in all
this time about the way those words are
fixed on brick with the same longing not
even the holiest stones mentioned in the
Bible keep. I finally return to thoughts
questioning how long America will treat
me like an unwanted guest on the land
that witnessed my birth? how long will
I feel her hate crimes on my scarred
flesh?

THE PLACE

the barrio is a place to see
children running games on the
street, old friends sitting around
an improvised table drinking ale
while playing dominoes, and for
walks touching the wrinkled hands
of abuelas with impatient dreams.
the barrio is where you write letters
to send thousands of miles away to
old lovers that remain in boxes and
tenement rooftops you climb to wait
for an ascending moon. the barrio is looking
out the fifth-floor window to see an elderly
Jewish fiddler telling the truth with Albinoni's
Adagio on a chilly morning leaving you filled
with homesickness. the barrio is the concrete
streets grasping Martin's dream in a world that
contests white fairy-tale logic and the once upon
a time spaces of a splintered and confused
nation.

WAR

there is silence before the rustling
leaves this morning, on the street
until someone yells for Miguelito to
come out, in the church that has not
started performing confession, in birds
waiting on branches of a quiet tree
for the sun to crash on them and in the
air not yet full of words. there is silence
in Ukraine with the death of speech, after
final lullabies and every lastly cradled
breath.

THE MARKET

walking to Tremont Avenue
from the community center
with my little sister I pointed to
the A&P saying I help elderly
Jewish ladies carry groceries
home and they tip me with a
quarter, and sometimes a few
pennies more. it was snowing
that day and the sidewalks made
that crunchy sound beneath each
step like it was trading hellos with
our cold feet inside of paper thin
shoes. we had several blocks yet
to walk before making it back to
the apartment where mother kept
an altar full of Saints to the God
of her dead relatives we never
knew. it was that time in the late
afternoon when the next group of
the poor headed to nightshift work
wearing yesterday's grimy clothes
thinking the Savior would not ever
rise from his tomb in a New York
winter.

SANTERIA

when I was eleven years old
visiting the Santeria hall with
more shouts than a Pentecostal
storefront church, I believed life
was determined by nothing more
than spells. the African Yoruba
Chango who traveled to Puerto
Rico in chains appeared weekly
on Intervale Avenue and when the
drumming, channeling, and advising
stopped the priestess never asked for a
single cent from the poor like church.
I sat with friends in the back of the hall
enjoying my child's world, curious
about the pure magic that was healing
broken souls like my mother and her
best friend Ana and waiting for what
was to come out of the smoky front
of the room, where a women dressed
in white was possessed by a God older
than Christ. these days full of much to
wish for find me looking over my shoulder
for the dancing, speeches and drumming
that cured things.

ROMEO Y JULIETA

in the moonlit alley known
by the two kids playing
at Romeo and Juliet while
living in tenements the young
boy went to look up at a window
hoping to hear the soft voice of
his new love who wore beauty like
a Miro painting. when he looked up
at her window, he could see more than
an Irish girl whose family attended the
English Mass in the same church that
kept Spanish speakers like him apart in
in the church basement. he was certain the
two shared a dream about their innocent
fugitive love. they heard too often at the
kitchen table they would be ambushed by
separating agents and never imagined it
would be difficult to love otherwise. in a
world too sick for their love, these kids saw
themselves in the shadows endlessly talking
and feeling close to the place ancient lovers
eternalized with song.

NO KNEELING

I lived like you a half life
on the streets, walking them
sideways, fluent with words
that shackled your voice, the
idea of family no more than
story-book pages remembered
now and then in the untended
ground of South Bronx graves.
I look for you today in places
where Christ still rises from the
dead, with people earning wages
too thin for three daily meals and
the faces of the kids rushing to
things they cannot change. I had
words from a psalm placed on your
headstone, recite prayers several
times a year by it to the God of
drying bones and think in quiet
times about tearing the good book
into two worthless halves to send
God a message about the world
and church that forgot you.

POLITICIANS

I live in a divided country that
does not read its centuries of
history, cannot be bothered with
bells of liberty and argues about
the color of God to shame even
the imagination that invented
deities in earliest Greece. I live
in a nation moving away from its
revolutionary truth, closer to the
terrorist States that delight when
people disappear and that cannot
stop from sending a plague of crosses
throughout the land so the scorned
make nothing happen. I live in a
place that builds big walls to keep
out those who are the witnesses of
hope and dream of life, liberty and
happiness. I spend my days in the
neighborhoods the Universities fail
to teach, where Jesus lives one door
away and blocks are saturated with
harsh spots never visited by the white
politicians who stupidly think God
is a conservative US citizen.

ADORED

only God can breathe freedom
on these streets, hear the feintest
prayers and let lose the wretched
bones kept in chains. only God
can keep us unafraid of the devils
urging sanctimonious politicians
and hateful white citizens to look
upon others without love. only God
can ask us to leave aside resentment,
to cast apart rage, find strength in
weakness and make room for grace.
only God can reach us in times that
lack meaning, in the bitter tragedies
stubbornly fashioning the world on
its terms, the callous indifference of
civilization and in the places convinced
by tears there is no hope. only with God
can silence be for us an act of presence, a
sign we learned noiseless prayer.

QUIETLY

love came one evening
with a gentle rain taking
me into its hand. the radio
played songs of care with
kisses carried by the wind
from the open window in a
corner of the room. it was
the first-time life happened
with approaching light and
songbirds sending delicious
notes. since then, I come to
life every day asking for a little
bit more to keep my glad heart
pounding. love came to me in
the dark of night and I shouted
come close, draw nearer to me
and whisper something sweet
with your everlasting lips.

THE PARK

in the park you notice
the faint music coming
from the direction of the
Bethesda Fountain that
often appears in movies.
a light breeze combs hair
on the homeless walking
the paths in no particular
direction and you think it
is a fine time to read a few
pages of Jorge Luis Borges
in a mad attempt to bring the
world into order temporary
though it may be. you near
the fading light of day watching
people make the Great Lawn
crossing, notice park lamps are
broken and sense for some odd
reason you want to ask people with
whom you share life for forgiveness.
you hear angelic Spanglish shouts
coming from a distance and thank
heaven for the benediction that requires
translation like the lines in the Holy
Book.

OLD TIMERS

start by talking to the old
timers on the corner who swear
there is a cure to being young.
every time you pause for a talk
with them you will hear they
sailed above trouble though
somewhat in a cloud. try talking
with the old man who has his
mother's name carved on one arm
and his brother's gravestone on the
other to remind himself of love on
earth like in heaven. the old timers
have lived in a dream that settled
in them the first day they saw the
urban landscape and imagined lamp
posts on the block palm trees with
enviable ease. they will take you to
places the news headlines have never
understood and tell you what a blessing
to feel the unpolished world with godly
kindness.

THE SHOP

you walk the Avenue until you
reach Southern Boulevard at the
point where the subway track is
curved, go down the block passed
the old men set up on the corner
beside the parking meters with shoe
shine boxes, and make your way for
two blocks to the little botanica next
to the Star movie house that has saintly
pictures, images of rebellious Angels
and African Gods on its walls staring
out the store window. the sun is shining
on the street though not warmly in the
early winter, you look through the door
of the botanica to see a woman doing
more things than time allows to prepare
an evening Santero meeting and children
play in front of the agonized face of Jesus
posed in porcelain. this shop is not Irish,
Italian or Jewish owned, never visited by
the uptown better off, speaks very little
english and is known as a place to shout
and dance with Middle Eastern, African
and rain Gods that sweep up burdens and
the curses of the poor.

COLLEGE TOWN

once in a little Ohio town
named All-American city
that turned off around eight
each night, I remember calling
home from a public phone and
suddenly surrounded by three
police cars with cops looking
straight at me. I thought nothing
of it until one came to me and
with his tongue said spic hang it
up. I was carted off to spend the
night in jail for no reason and
nearly suffocated on the white
supremacy of the college town
police and the silence of a school
dean who was told what happened
to me by the white boy on the same
evening walk who did not suffer a
damn thing!

THE SPELL

the crying spells come
with little reason in the
world that cannot teach
them to be silent. they
never learned to speak
English, yet hear a mother's
whispers and always shed
for those laid quietly in a
box. the tears come out
despite myself from places
where bunched up sorrow
pushes out while I stare out
apartment windows beneath
which the junkies gather no
longer thinking of nagging love
with words. when names come
near like sticks and stones that
break bones the crying spells return
making me shout Jesus you called
forth the dead now draw near!

DROPS

we are the children who invented
rap in forgotten neighborhoods,
beaten by cops, trashed in school,
deserted by fathers, described like
criminals, destroyed by dope and
dying too young. we are the kids
that know nothing about the liberty
bell, those who speak Spanglish in
prison for stealing a meal and have
no say in a despising world. we are
the children rejected in church, living
in abandoned tenements, shanty-town
lots, subway stations, beneath bridges
and in parks. we are the children alive
each hour with affluent hearts, making
up words like geniuses and watching
each other violently go into graves. we
are the children not mended, replaying by
the hour the sins of those who wake up
each day plain dead, and the ones who
may find a way someday to say you are
forgiven.

ALWAYS EXILE

they left with no intention of
ever going back wearing new
shoes they planned to wear out
on the sidewalks and until the
wood floors in the apartments
white families long ago fled are
stripped of stain. the lush green
mountains call out to them and the
rivers shout their names while they
go on spilling tears for places that
cannot reclaim them, they will never
admit living with no return, always
claim to be no more than temporary
exiles, lament the rearing of children
who forget Spanish a little more each
year and remain in a state of strangeness
in the country that loathes them though is
always ready to exploit them. they weep
hearing the praises for a former president
who sent military aid to a tiny nation despite
the pleading from a priest made a Saint.
they will always pray a reckoning like the
good book title written by the habitat man
and ex-president whose hands are stained by
the blood of a different Holy land!

THE NEW POLITICS

there is no attempt made to hide
the delusional narratives that pour
out of the mouths of elected officials
like potent truth and they speak more
loudly of everything there is to fear.
truth is nothing more today than a word
to slice tongues, an English noun pleading
for sanity by people beaten to the ground
by those who chant hate, today, Satan, it
appears drives the new politics and
citizens who walk the streets in silence
cry themselves awake at night afraid to
denounce the hissing witness producing
the stench of a republic slowly and surely
turning to rot. dark, darker still is the city
set on a hill, dim, dimmer yet is the beacon
of light once clearly seen on the other side
of the world. here sweet Emma on the sea
washed shores you well know the mighty
woman's flame is out, her lips silent and
the authoritarian thugs have crawled out
from beneath the rocks to make sickening
rounds.

FISHING

Shorty loved to fish eels at a
favorite spot off a pier at Hunts
Point Market where he would
sit the day without ever hearing a
school bell ring. every now and
then he touched the rosary kept in
a pocket given to him by an Irish
priest who blessed cops each year
before the Saint Patrick Day Parade
in Manhattan saying it has saving
power though it could not prevent
arsonists from burning abandoned
buildings on the block or torching
churches that locked their doors to
keep junkies out. often, he sat at
the water's edge thinking about the
many times he ate God in Mass waiting
for magic to happen then saying it
was absent because he forgot to say
please. Shorty would sit there fishing
enjoying every weakness in him for which
a Crucified darker brother had prepared
gifts and feeling no shame for being a
spic.

BELOVED

the rose was never more
beautiful than when I stood
beside you in a moment far
bigger than experience and
seconds frailer than any crisp
Autumn leaves. something
about you through these many
years is more precious than any
dream, the sun that warms new
days and the wind that carries your
voice into places far and near. you
have always been unspeakably true
like everlasting love and I confess
with you mystery has become mine
for keeps.

SIT

come sit with me by
the fire lighting the
dark night, talk with me
about the things you
care, hear the crickets
singing to each other,
and gaze at nothing in
particular with frantic
love. come let me hear
your voice deafening
the unwelcome, recalling
each memory held with
elation, offering tender words
like bread for life and bewildering
crooked streets. come sit here
until we hear children in the
summer evening laughing on
the sidewalks. come let us
whisper with hearts swung
open and declared fulfilled.

MOTHER

I miss the simple things like
the record player that spun
78 vinyl records with little
Anthony tunes and El Gran
Combo on Saturday morning
with the smell of King Pine in
the living room rising from the
linoleum floor. you a young
single mother working magic
for three kids, lost for hours
singing to Saints, African and
Taíno Gods that helped clean
away the city dust in our two
room apartment. I miss those
trousers you got me for school
that I outgrew until they were the
best puddle jumpers in the Bronx,
the shoes with holes we stuffed
with cardboard that you said never
wear to knell in church and the
trips to the wide strip of Orchard
Beach with your girlfriends to dig
in the sand, eat fried chicken and
spend the day combing the grounds
for deposit bottles to return to 1203
with chump change. I can see you
still smiling in the Bronx, beneath
a palm tree in Puerto Rico, the day
Rudy made his first communion and
in that place in me that will never let
you go. I have carried you for these
many years after your ashes were
scattered in the wind dear mother

and buried with tender Spanish deep
within me.

CHINESE LAUNDRY

the block party started
when Willy Lee whose
mother owned a Chinese
Hand Laundry shop told
friends from the basement
of his soul they would be
moving to Chinatown in
Manhattan. they were tired
of the twelve-pound iron, the
14-hour days, shelving starched
shirts, clean sheets and steamed
heat fabrics. Willy wanted to
be a doctor in his dreams not a
USA born laundryman checking
dirty clothes and day-after-day
getting them ready for ironing,
sorting, packing, pickup and
sleeping in a backroom. the sky
was blue the day of the block
party, pigeons gathered in front
of the Lee Laundry store eating
tiny pieces of bread left on the
sidewalk and Willy's mother
out shaking her head told Lela
who was sitting on a milk crate
in front of the Perez bodega no
more wash clothes to make them
dance. the Lee family was moving
to an undecorated future by Canal
Street where tea tasted like the old
Yangtze River and they could count
the things no longer needed to
turn the pages on dreams.

THEODICY

they come to me at night
with a candle burning on
my desk, the thoughts of
the sweet theologians that
have spoken to me over a
near spent lifetime and I
puzzle over their words
that save for a few have
not kept their feet on the
ground. I must wonder with
Milosz about the morality of
God in a world these thinkers
swear is fallen and having a bit
more faith does not explain how
divine love overcomes injustice,
inequity, the condition of the poor
and oppressed suffering. I sit up at
night asking the books written by
theologians how cultures of cruelty,
the carnage left by guns, the death of
the innocent, the arrogance of the rich,
and the indifference of politicians is not
a plague of biblical proportion? I weep
in my country about how God is regularly
killed, while the poor go on telling the Lord
they wish to be more than burnt offerings to
the earth, and live.

www.ingramcontent.com/pod-product-compliance
Lightning Source LLC
LaVergne TN
LVHW020626100826
845148LV00012B/2064

* 9 7 8 1 6 6 6 7 7 5 1 2 9 *